Piano Practice and Performance

✦ Achieve your full potential on the piano

✦ Enhance memory & performance skills

✦ For students & aspiring professionals

Barry & Linda Wehrli

Piano Practice and Performance

 The letter C with a circle around it stands for the word **copyright**.

Copyright is made up of two words:
Copy: To make a picture of or create another of something.
Right: Permission to own, create or use something.

The copyright on this book protects the rights of its publisher to copy, sell, give away, make changes in, or publicly show the book to others. To do so without the publisher's written permission violates the publisher's rights.

The **copyright notice** is the copyright symbol, the date of publication, and the name of the publisher, as shown at the top of this page.

Wehrli Publications

Educational Music & Art
Products for the Professional
Teacher and Retailer

12830 Burbank Boulevard, Box 204
Valley Village, CA 91607-1402
www.wehrlipubs.com

Cover designed by Sandy Fox, eMedia Solutions, Inc.   Photographic modeling provided by Corey Bridwell.

Foreword

Have you. . .

- Typically played pieces from beginning to end *just to get through* them?

- Ignored recurring mistakes without taking the time to correct them, hoping to *eventually* get it right?

- Set aside a challenging piece in favor of easier music?

- Procrastinated your practice until just before the lesson?

- Not met your progress or performance expectations?

These are symptoms of incorrect or no practice technique. Left unhandled, they erode interest and enthusiasm until, eventually, one has "reasonable" justifications for quitting.

If any of the above sounds familiar, use this book to get back on track.

Piano Practice and Performance is a collection of helpful and concise tips on correct practice techniques and performance strategies, researched and tested by the authors in their own practices. Use these tips to improve your music studies and confidence at the piano.

Our goal is to assist the piano student in achieving a rewarding, aesthetic hobby or career, and to help instructors guide their students accordingly.

Golden Rule of Practice

- Practice does *not* make perfect.
- *Correct* practice makes perfect and permanent.

About the Authors

Barry Wehrli began piano and keyboard studies at the age of eight. His formal training includes instruction from Dolores Rhoads, Terry Trotter and John Novello and music studies at California State University, Northridge. He composes, arranges and records at his home studio, is a freelance performer, heads Wehrli Publications and teaches piano and electronic music. His clients include Warner Brothers, Yamaha, and local professional musicians and teachers.

Linda Wehrli has been soloing and accompanying on the piano since the age of six. Her teachers include Esther Lee Caplan, Mario Feninger and John Novello. The skills gained while earning her Bachelor's of Science Degree in Business Administration from California State University, Northridge helped her build a successful music and art teaching academy, Pastimes for a Lifetime, Inc.

How to use this Book

- In addition to the many practice and performance tips presented here, additional tips from your instructor can be noted on the Instructor's Suggestions form on page 59.

- Practice tips are listed by chapter in the Table of Contents. Read Chapters 1 and 2 in the order presented and use Chapters 3 and 4 for specific needs.

- Make sure all words, symbols and concepts are fully understood. Use a dictionary to clear up words as you read.

- A glossary of musical terms is presented on pages 53 - 57.

- If a confusion occurs, return to the appropriate section of the book and look for a misunderstood word or symbol in that area. If it cannot be found there, search earlier or later until you find the misunderstood word or symbol. Use a dictionary to clear up all of its definitions, using each in sentences. Then restudy from that point forward in the text. Repeat as needed, until the problem is resolved.

Piano Practice and Performance

Table of Contents

Piano Practice and Performance

Chapter 1

Practice Defined

Webster's Collegiate dictionary defines "practice" in the following order:

1. *to perform or work at repeatedly so as to become proficient*
In the developing stages of musicianship, you *perform or work at your music studies repeatedly to become proficient*, developing necessary mental and physical skills.

2. *to do or perform often, customarily, or habitually*
When you *do or perform often, customarily, or habitually*, piano practice is part of your daily routine, allowing the time needed to advance in your studies and musicianship.

3. *to be professionally engaged in (as in practicing medicine, law, etc.)*
Diligence at definitions one and two is the path to becoming a professional musician.

The order in which these definitions are presented is also the order by which students can achieve their musical goals, through practice.

Your Purpose for Practicing

Being able to understand and play professional-level piano gives a sense of fulfillment and satisfaction, even if a career in music is not being pursued. When listening to music or observing a virtuoso performance that fills one with awe and exhilaration, we are the *effect* of the music. Imagine what it would be like to be the *cause* of that awe and exhilaration - to reach the ability level of the musicians who have inspired us, and then cause that feeling in others and ourselves.

Before you begin studying the piano, follow these steps:

1. Decide to *be* a pianist, regardless of your current ability level. This is the foundation of your involvement with music. Stay true to your intention - it is the fuel that will keep you going.

2. Ensure the intention to be a pianist is yours and yours alone. It must come from within, not from others pushing you to be something that you do not want to be.

3. Keep your focus. Do not let the problems of life overshadow your musical goals.

4. Be wary of people who discourage your piano goals in the guise of being concerned for your well-being, perhaps suggesting you should do something that "isn't so risky" or "will earn you a better living". Your goals belong to you.

Our goal with this book is to help you achieve *your* goals.

Your Practice Schedule

INVOLVEMENT

Regular practice means to dedicate a *minimum* of five days a week to your piano studies. The frequency of exposure to and level of involvement with your studies determines your progress. Immerse yourself fully, not superficially. Lasting results are achieved by consistent practice.

1. Discuss your practice schedule with family and friends. Ask for their support to see that your practice time is respected and no one feels compromised.

2. If studying with an instructor, schedule regular lessons allowing ample time to practice between each lesson. Lessons are typically scheduled once a week.

3. Frequent shorter sessions produce better results than less frequent longer sessions. For example, five consecutive days of 30-minute practice sessions are preferred over two or three sporadic 1-hour sessions.

4. Schedule your practice time to be equal to or greater than your lesson time. If your lesson is one hour, plan to practice a minimum of one hour.

5. If you practice on an acoustic piano, have it tuned regularly. Most technicians recommend a tuning every six months and at that frequency other maintenance issues can be discovered and handled before they become a hinderance to your practice.

6. Plan time to dust or clean your piano, acoustic or electric. (See the owner's manual.)

INSTRUCTION FORMS

To keep your studies on track, use the following two forms:
1. A study plan of assignments and targets for the week.
2. A calendar reminding you of the times you have set aside for piano practice.

Our **Music Instruction Forms: 1-Year Journal** contains forms for recording assignments and study progress over the course of one year. It is available for purchase at www.wehrlipubs.com or at selected retailers. See samples on the next page. These two forms will be referred to in the coming text.

When your Weekly Practice Calendar and Weekly Lesson Plan are set up, proceed to Chapter 2. If special needs arise, follow the advice in Chapter 3. When ready to memorize or perform music, refer to Chapter 4.

Wehrli Publications
Weekly Practice Calendar

- Choose 5 or more days per week to practice.
- The total daily practice time should be equal to or greater than the lesson time.

MONDAY		AM
		PM
TUESDAY		AM
		PM
WEDNESDAY		AM
		PM
THURSDAY		AM
		PM
FRIDAY		AM
		PM
SATURDAY		AM
		PM
SUNDAY		AM
		PM

TOTAL HOURS PER WEEK ☐

Wehrli Publications
Weekly Lesson Plan

DATE:_____

TECHNIQUE & EXERCISES

Order Quantity

☐ minutes
☐ repetitions   GRADE:

☐ minutes
☐ repetitions   GRADE:

☐ minutes
☐ repetitions   GRADE:

RHYTHM & EAR TRAINING

☐ minutes
☐ repetitions   GRADE:

☐ minutes
☐ repetitions   GRADE:

☐ minutes
☐ repetitions   GRADE:

THEORY & OTHER ACTIVITIES

☐ minutes
☐ repetitions   GRADE:

☐ minutes
☐ repetitions   GRADE:

☐ minutes
☐ repetitions   GRADE:

MUSIC & SIGHT-READING

☐ minutes
☐ repetitions   GRADE:

☐ minutes
☐ repetitions   GRADE:

☐ minutes
☐ repetitions   GRADE:

Piano Practice and Performance

Chapter 2

Music Preparation

Intellectual and perceptual preparations are necessary to understand the structure, texture and interpretation of a new piece. Prepare new music away from the keyboard, where you can listen and absorb the piece without the distraction of making the fingers work. Whether you are a beginner or seasoned player, use these tips *before* practice begins.

Note:

For classical music, obtain an Urtext edition, if possible. Urtext editions are closest to the composer's original instructions and intentions.

1. **Listen to professional recordings or live performances of the piece while following along with the score.** At the lesson, your instructor's performance and/or directions can be recorded for reference back home. Note what you like or dislike in each rendition of the piece. Each recording reflects interpretations of the music which may conflict with certain indications in your printed edition. Since you will eventually develop your own interpretation of the piece, avoid imitating or becoming dependent on *any* source.

2. **Find and make note of the key signature and time signature.**

3. **Find or determine the tempo mark.** If none is given, determine the tempo by listening to a recording with the metronome. If no recording is available, consult a qualified instructor or performer, or research it through your local library or the internet. Then write in the tempo mark at the beginning of the music.

4. **Locate the melodic phrases.** Plan to practice these sections separately since melodic phrases tend to be the most important part of a composition.

5. **Identify the scales, chords and form of the music, if possible.** Knowledge of these elements will greatly improve your understanding of the music.

Practice Session Setup

1. **Be well fed and well rested.**

2. **Eliminate distractions in your practice space.** Turn off all phones, beepers, radios, televisions, and so forth. Hang a "Do Not Disturb" sign on your door, if needed.

3. **Adjust the lighting in the room and over the piano desk to avoid eye strain.**

4. **Set up and test your recording equipment (tape or digital recorder, camcorder, etc.).**

5. **Have a sharpened pencil and eraser available for notations on the music.**

Stretches and Warm-Ups

Stretches and warm-ups prevent injury and keep your body relaxed and energized during practice. Keep the following points in mind:

- Make sure the muscles are warm before doing any stretches.
- Maintain relaxed, deep breathing throughout.
- Repeat each stretch as desired. However, this routine should last *no longer than ten percent* of your total practice time.
- Do stretches during and after lengthy practice sessions.

NECK AND SHOULDER STRETCHES

1. A. Gently lower your chin toward your chest as you exhale until the muscles stop your movement. Hold the stretch for a few seconds. Then inhale as you release back up.
   B. Repeat, gently raising your head back, toward the spine. Breathe and hold as indicated.

2. A. Slowly turn your head to the right as you exhale until the muscles stop your movement. Hold the stretch for a few seconds. Then inhale as you return back to center.
   B. Repeat, slowly turning your head to the left. Breathe and hold as indicated.

3. A. Gently tilt your head to the right (shoulder relaxed) as you exhale until the muscles stop your movement. Hold the stretch for a few seconds. Inhale as you return to center.
   B. Repeat, gently tilting your head to the left. Breathe and hold as indicated.

4. A. Lift your right shoulder towards your ear (head straight) as you exhale until the muscles stop your movement. Hold the stretch for a few seconds. Inhale as you release down.
   B. Repeat with your left shoulder. Breathe and hold as indicated.

FOREARM STRETCHES

1. A. Lift your right arm in front of the body, elbow straight, palm facing up.
   B. Grasp the right palm with the left hand, placing the left thumb underneath the right wrist.
   C. With the left hand, slowly lower the right hand, keeping the right elbow straight, until the muscles stop your movement. *Do not force the hand.* Release after five seconds.
   D. Repeat with the left arm.

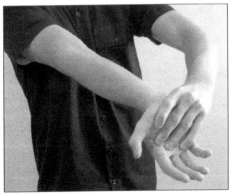

2. A. Lift your right arm in front of the body, elbow straight, palm facing down.
   B. Grasp the right hand with the left, placing the left thumb underneath the right wrist.
   C. With the left hand, slowly lower the right hand, keeping the right elbow straight, until the muscles stop your movement. *Do not force the hand.* Release after five seconds.
   D. Repeat with the left arm.

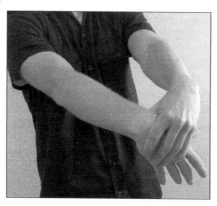

FINGER STRETCH

A. Lift your right arm in front of the body, elbow bent, palm facing down.
B. Spread fingers 2 and 3 apart, finger 2 pointing forward and the other fingers down.
C. Insert fingers 1 and 2 of the left hand between fingers 2 and 3 of the right hand, at the mid-joint (first joint after the knuckles). Keep the left fingers straight, right fingers relaxed.
D. Gently spread apart fingers 2 and 3 of the right hand, using the two left fingers.
E. Reverse the right-hand fingers (finger 2 pointing down and the other fingers forward).
F. Insert fingers 1 and 2 of the left hand between fingers 2 and 3 of the right hand, at the mid-joint and spread them apart. Keep the left fingers straight, right fingers relaxed.
G. Repeat steps A - F with each adjacent pair of fingers in each hand, except fingers 1 and 2.

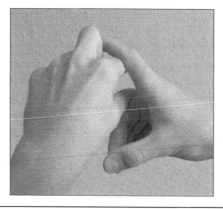 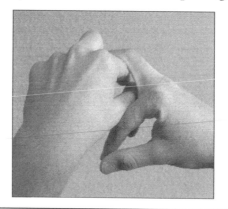

FINGER WARM-UP (EXERCISE BALLS)

Four-inch diameter, foam rubber exercise balls are recommended for this warm-up.
They should be soft enough to squeeze but firm enough to return to their original shape.
These balls are sold separately and can be purchased at www.wehrlipubs.com. ——————→

A. Hold an exercise ball firmly in each hand.

B. Stand or sit so both arms hang loosely at your sides. Do *not* bend your elbows or wrists.

C. Squeeze both balls at the same time, curving all fingertips as if to make a fist with each squeeze. Do this until your hands feel tired, but not sore. Note the number of squeezes you have done.

D. Do this amount *before* every practice session. Each week, increase the number of daily squeezes by 5 or 10, depending on your ability level, never allowing the hands to become sore. Example: First week, do 40 squeezes at the start of each practice session. Second week, do 50 squeezes. Third week, do 60, etc.

E. When you can do 200 squeezes daily, maintain this amount. Going beyond 200 squeezes is optional, as long as the hands do not become sore.

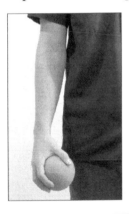

Correct

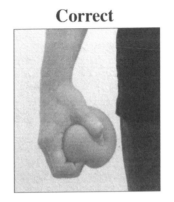

Incorrect

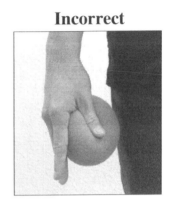

LOWER BACK AND LEG STRETCH

Do this stretch after sitting at the piano for an extended period of time.

A. Stand with your feet about shoulder width apart, legs straight but knees not locked.

B. Place your hands on your hips.

C. Arch your lower back with your buttocks pointing out.

D. Slowly lower your torso forward as you exhale, keeping the lower back arched and neck straight with the torso. Continue until the rear leg muscles stop your movement.

E. Hold the stretch for a few seconds. Do not bounce.

F. Bend the knees slightly and slowly raise the torso back up as you inhale.

KEYBOARD TECHNIQUE TIPS

1. **Warm up to fast technical exercises by playing them at a slower, more relaxed tempo.** This avoids straining muscles not yet conditioned for immediate and demanding playing.

2. **Do not work on all technical exercises collectively.** Spread them out among your various projects to prevent fatigue.

3. **Relate technique to your music. First, play a technical exercise that requires the ability called for in a piece, then play that piece.** This reinforces application. Remember this when organizing the assignments on your Weekly Lesson Plan.

Basic Posture at the Piano

Correct posture at the piano improves the quality of your playing and can prevent discomfort and injury. Basic Posture as shown below, is the starting point which should become habit. A qualified instructor might recommend slight adjustments depending on musical context.

1. Pull out and center the bench parallel to the keyboard. See figures 1 and 3.

2. Sit on the front half of the bench. Do not sit all the way back. See figure 2.

3. Center your body in front of the middle D key (next to middle C).
   Maintain this seated position regardless of where you play on the keyboard. See figure 3.

Fig. 1 - Incorrect

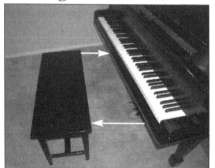

Fig. 2 - Correct

Fig. 3 - Correct

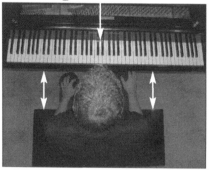

4. Keeping your lower back and shoulders straight, lean forward slightly. See figure 4A.
   Keep shoulders relaxed, not in a shrug. See figures 4B and 4C.

Fig. 4A - Correct

Fig. 4B - Correct

Fig. 4C - Incorrect

5. Rest the fingertips on the white keys directly in front of you. Elbows should rest near the front of your torso, not ahead of or behind the torso. Adjust the bench accordingly.
   This determines the *correct distance* to sit from the keyboard. Keep in mind step 2, above.

Correct

Incorrect

Seated *too far* from the keyboard.

Incorrect

Seated *too close* to the keyboard.

6. Forearms should be level, not angled up or down. Lower or raise the bench or use a flat cushion, accordingly. This determines the *correct height* of the piano bench.

Correct

Incorrect

Seated *too low*.

Seated *too high*.

7. Upper legs and knees should be clear of the keyboard.

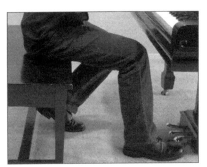

8. Rest the right foot on the floor near the right pedal. Rest the left foot behind the right, as shown below. This maintains balance. Correct posture and movement when using the pedals is covered in Chapter 3, page 27.

Correct

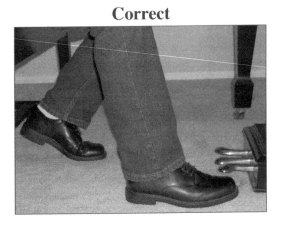

Incorrect

9. If your feet do not reach the floor, rest them on a footstool. Feet should be flat and side-by-side on the surface with knees clear of the piano. Do not dangle feet in the air.

10. Adjust the piano desk for easy music reading. This basic step prevents eye strain and posture problems.

11. **Wrists are held flat or parallel to the keyboard.** Do not drop your wrists below the keyboard. Never yank wrists up and down.

Correct	Incorrect	Incorrect
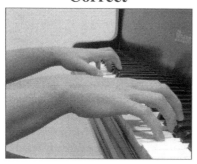		

12. **Thumbs stay on the keyboard at an angle to the keys.** Do not lift your thumbs above or drop them below the keyboard.

Correct	Correct	Incorrect
		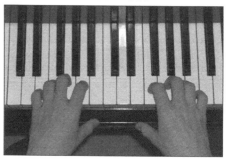

13. **Rest the thumbs and pinky fingers closer to the edge of the keys.** Place the other fingers near the center of the white keys. (See pictures, above.)

14. **Curve fingers 2-5 as if holding a ball.** Keep these finger joints curved while playing (unless a reach demands a straightening of the fingers). Avoid letting the *nail joints* collapse backwards, toward you. Keep nails trimmed at or behind the finger pad.

Correct	Correct Key Press	Incorrect Key Press
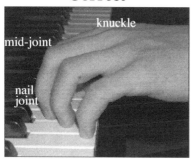	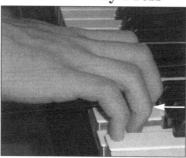	

15. **Keep finger movements minimal and relaxed.** When lifting up keys, keep fingers on the key surface as much as possible. Avoid bouncing fingers off the keys.

16. **Before playing, relax all muscles in the body except those needed to support the head, lower back and wrists.** Do not clench your teeth, shrug the shoulders, tighten the legs or buttocks, etc.

17. **Keep your head still while playing.** Do not bob your head to the beats.

3X Rule (3 *Times* Rule)

Repetition increases awareness while practicing. It takes several times through a small section or phrase to thoroughly understand and be able to play it consistently without error. Practicing with the 3X Rule reinforces correct playing and sets an immediate goal to reach, reducing frustration and exhaustion.

Procedure:

A. Repeat a small section or phrase section until you play it correctly two times in a row.

B. Close your eyes and play the area once again. If there were errors of any kind, repeat A and B until there are none. If no errors were made, go on to the next Practice Routine step.

Important Note:

In steps 2-9 of the following Practice Routine, the 3X Rule determines the completion of *each* step.

Practice Routine

Follow these steps to enhance your practice sessions and reinforce good practice habits.

Notes:
- **If your reading skills are sufficient to allow it, sight-read the piece once through to get an idea of the piece's character and structure. Then begin these steps.**
- **The Practice Routine steps are presented in our recommended order. Your instructor may change the order at his or her discretion, as long as the end result is the same - an aesthetic and accurate performance.**

1. **Determine how much of the piece you want to work on.** Select one section or phrase which fulfills your practice session goal and avoids overwhelm.

2. **Play the first section, hands separately, learning the notes, beats and fingering.** (Alternating-hand patterns should be learned hands together.)
   A. **Establish a "base tempo" (see glossary).**
   B. **Make fingering notations or corrections, as needed.** (See Chapter 3 - Visual Guides and Fingering, pages 22-24.)

3. **At your base tempo, learn all articulation and dynamic markings.** Avoid the rote tendency to speed up when playing louder or slow down when playing softer, unless indicated by the music or your instructor. Use the metronome if needed.

4. **Gradually work each hand up to the speed indicated by the tempo mark.** Use the metronome if needed. Keep in mind that the metronome is not a crutch and that you will need to keep the final tempo flowing without it.

5. **Add tempo changes as indicated in the music.** Avoid beginning a change of tempo at the start of a phrase or measure. Start at a later point, preferably on a weak beat to avoid an abrupt or anxious sound.

6. **Add pedaling as indicated in the music.** Pedaling with hands separately helps you focus on correct foot movement and hear the effect of pedaling on each hand.

7. **Play the first section with hands together at a base tempo.** Expressive aspects such as articulation, dynamics and so forth may be excluded temporarily for the sake of developing hand coordination, but should be returned before speed is increased.

8. **Gradually work up to the speed indicated by the tempo mark.** If the metronome is used, remember that you will need to keep the final tempo flowing without it while observing any tempo changes.

9. **Play the section at tempo mark speed, focusing on the final touches of correct phrasing and voice balancing.**

10. **Practice the next section of the piece using steps 1-9. Join together sections that have been completed** *per these steps.* Go on to a new section when the current one can be played easily with the following applicable points correctly executed:

  - Posture
  - Fingering
  - Note pitches

  - Note durations
  - Rest durations
  - Articulation

  - Dynamics
  - Phrasing
  - Voice balance

  - Overall tempo
  - Tempo changes
  - Pedaling

11. **Near the bottom of a page, determine the point where one hand is available to turn the page. Memorize the surrounding area so that the music can continue, uninterrupted by the page turn.**

12. **When the entire piece is learned, record your performance. Listen to your recording, following along with the score to check the above points.** Make sure you have carried out all notations made. A recording provides a more objective viewpoint of your progress. Are technical and expressive aspects developing along intended goals? If not, make corrections accordingly and re-record your performance. Your interpretation of the piece should be guided by a solid understanding of the music, the composer's intention and the stylistic tendencies of the era in which the piece was written.

Ending the Session

Before leaving the piano, do the following to keep the gains obtained during the session and motivate you to come back for more.

1. **Evaluate your progress.** Compare the goals set by your instructor or yourself with the progress made in the session. Keep in mind you are building *perceptions* as well as skills. Notice any changes in your perceptions and abilities.

2. **Keep a positive perspective of your musical abilities.** If you compare yourself to other, more advanced players, be inspired, not discouraged.

3. **Reward yourself by playing anything you like.**
   - One of your favorite songs.
   - An improvisation.
   - An unknown piece (using the sight-reading tips on page 36).
   - A song heard on the radio or a recording.
   Do not "practice to get it right"; just enjoy yourself.

4. **Remember to stretch if you have been sitting for a while.** (See Stretches and Warm-Ups, pages 10-12.)

Piano Practice and Performance

Chapter 3 - Special Cases

Handling Problem Spots

Problem spot: A recurring mistake or the same mistake made *twice* (two instances of the same mistake means it *is* recurring). Do not ignore a problem spot, believing it will go away if you "get it right once", or if you "just keep playing". Doing so will only ingrain the mistake.

Use the procedure below to correct a problem spot.

1. Determine *exactly* what and where the mistake is in the music.
2. Find an easy starting point that leads you into the mistake.
3. Select an appropriate ending point that takes you just past the mistake.

With the practice area defined, apply one or more of the following tips:

- **Reduce the tempo.**
  A. Find the metronome speed at which you have been trying to play the area.

  B. Adjust the metronome two or more speeds lower until you find the speed at which no mistakes are made, on the *first* try. Note this speed as your base tempo (see glossary).

  C. Use the 3X Rule to perfect the area at base tempo.

  D. *Gradually* raise the metronome speed. At each successive speed, if you play the area correctly on the first try, immediately advance to the next speed. At any speed where a mistake is made on the first attempt, use the 3X Rule *at that speed*, then advance to the next higher speed. Continue this procedure until you arrive back at your original tempo.

- **Separate the hands.** If playing hands together is too difficult even at slower speeds, review one hand at a time using steps C and D above. When ready, put the hands back together and follow steps B - D above.

- **Count out loud.** This helps organize and coordinate the hands and fingers for that area.

Note:
If a recurring mistake will not resolve, do the following:
1. Make sure you fully understand all words, symbols and concepts in the music.
2. Check the topics in Chapter 3 to see if any apply to your situation. If an applicable topic is found, practice it with the above tips in mind.
3. Consult your instructor or another professional for advice.
4. Consider if the piece you are working on is beyond your ability level.

Visual Guides

Visual guides are notes made in the music as a reminder to do or not do something. They are helpful when learning new music. With the possible exception of fingering, use visual guides sparingly, as they are not a substitute for proper attention to printed detail.

• Select words or symbols that communicate clearly to you.
• Write your visual guides in pencil so they can be altered or erased, as needed.

Examples of typical notations are shown below.

• Write a reminder to check the key signature (until it becomes a habit).

• Write in necessary fingerings.

• Circle missed dynamic marks.

• Write in beats that are difficult to count, (not to be confused with fingering).

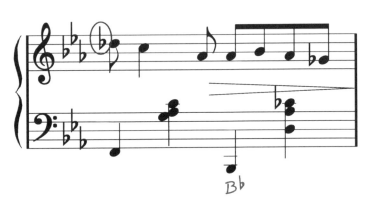

• Circle missed accidentals.

• Write in ledger line notes that are difficult to remember or recognize.

Fingering

Fingering not only determines which fingers to use in playing the keys, but is essential to correct expression and memorization.

FINGERING RULES

1. **The printed fingering in any publication may or may not be correct.** Corrections or additions may be needed according to Rules 2 and 3 below.

2. **Correct phrasing is senior to ease of fingering.** Use fingering which follows the composer's expressive intention (if known) and best supports all printed articulation.

3. **Only if the performer's hand size cannot fulfill the intended fingering can Rule 2 be compromised.**

4. **Concentrate on one hand at a time.** After correct fingering is determined and can be played well at your base tempo, gradually work that hand up to the final speed.

5. **Once a fingering is determined, stay with it so it becomes routine and eventually part of your tactile memory.** (More at Tactile Memory, page 42.)

Ask these questions when researching fingering:
- Is your hand making extraneous motions to get through the passage?
- Should the thumb cross under the hand or should the whole hand shift?
- Should a finger cross over the thumb? Which finger? Or should the whole hand shift?
- Does a finger need to slide off a black key to an adjacent white key?
- Does a finger need to play two adjacent keys when the hand stretches wide?
- If a note seems unreachable in one hand, can fingering be adjusted for its inclusion?
- If one hand straddles the other, which hand should be on top? What fingers will be least in the way?

In the example below, four fingerings are given. All end correctly, placing the 5th finger on the G in measure 4. With your right hand, try out these fingerings to determine which ones convey good phrasing.

melody from Jesu, Joy of Man's Desiring
J. S. Bach

Below are two fingerings for the same three-measure passage of a Beethoven Bagatelle. Play the right hand part of each example to feel the difference between them. Observe the slur markings over each group of two eighth notes. These markings indicate why the first fingering is correct and the second is not.

measures 45-47 - Elf Neue Bagatellen 1, Opus 119
Ludwig Von Beethoven

Correct Fingering

Incorrect Fingering

Additional Tips:

- **Use the strong fingers (1, 2 and 3) for louder accents, notes requiring a heavy tone or when clear articulation is needed.**

- **Scales accustom us to use long fingers on the black keys and short fingers on the white keys. However, musical sections might require that the thumb or pinky finger be used on black keys, to fulfill correct phrasing.**

- **Use the same fingering for each repetition of a phrase, if possible.** This prevents confusion of the phrases. If the same phrase occurs in two different keys, use a single fingering that works best for both phrases, in both keys.

- **When the same phrase or passage appears in a different octave, use the same fingering for both.**

- **Avoid changing fingers on repeated notes of three or more.** This keeps the arm in position for what follows. At or near the end of the repetitions, a shift may be needed to prepare for the next position. As you play the repetition, move the arm slightly toward or away from the keyboard, causing the fingertip to strike the key in a different place with each stroke. This creates a sense of melodic direction. Cycle through the fingers (e.g. 3,2,1,3,2,1 . . .) if the repetition speed is too great for the arm or hand to manage.

For more information on this important subject, refer to the books listed in our bibliography or consult a qualified piano instructor.

Reaching Techniques

Follow these points when the arms or fingers span a large area of the keyboard.

- **When you approach either end of the keyboard, lean your upper body to that side and move slightly forward.** Stay seated while moving your upper body. Do *not* scoot around on the bench. Your torso should curve towards the piano at either end.

- **When both hands are at the upper end (far right) of the keyboard, place the left foot to the left of the pedals.** This maintains your balance. Practice leaning the upper body to the right as described above, and moving your left foot to the left to get a sense of how these two motions work together.

Leaning to the Right

- **When both hands are at the lower end (far left) of the keyboard, tuck the left foot behind the right foot.** This keeps your balance and allows the right foot access to the pedal. Practice leaning the upper body to the left as described above, and moving the left foot behind the right to get a sense of how these two motions work together.

Leaning to the Left

- **When the upper body needs to lunge forward, such as when playing loudly, place the left foot underneath the bench.** This keeps your balance as the weight of your upper body bears down on the keys.

Lunge Forward

- **When a hand must jump from one part of the keyboard to another, do the following:**
  1. Memorize the measure before and after the jump.
  2. Move the hand in an arch *over* the keyboard. Prepare the fingers in mid air before falling on the target note(s). This is especially true with chords, whose "shape" should be in the fingers long before they arrive on the keyboard.
  3. Move back and forth slowly and continuously between the two areas of the jump, using the 3X Rule.
  4. Using a metronome, gradually raise the speed to the final tempo of the piece, using the 3X Rule at each higher speed.

- **Hand size may require special consideration in reaching large chords. Consider one of the following:**
  A. **Transfer one or more notes to the other hand.** In the example below, the left-hand D is transferred to the right hand where it is easier to play.

  B. **Omit duplicate notes in the chord.** Below, the right-hand F is omitted, eliminating the need to stretch the hand. Since an F already exists in the left hand, the character and function of the chord is maintained.

  C. **Roll the chord.** Rolling chords allows the student to capture the notes in a chord without having to strike them simultaneously; the notes are quickly "layered in". Usually, rolled chords anticipate the beat on which they occur. The last note of the roll occurs *on* the beat with prior notes being layered in near the end of the previous beat. However it is done, the speed and direction (up or down) of the roll should fit the form of the passage in which it occurs and also preserve the underlying rhythm.
  - If a chord is *not* notated as a roll or arpeggio, then transferring notes or omitting duplicate notes may be preferable, as these retain the intended sounding of the chord.

The Piano Pedals

Soft (Una Corda) Pedal →   ← Damper Pedal

Sostenuto Pedal

The damper pedal is the most commonly used pedal on the piano. This pedal raises the dampers (see glossary) off the strings, allowing the sound to continue after the keys are released.

PEDALING RULES

- **Align your foot with the pedal, resting the ball of your foot on the pedal edge.** If you have small feet, place your toes on the pedal edge, *not* the ball of your foot, allowing your heel to remain on the floor.

- **Keep your heel on the floor at all times, using it as a pivot point while a pedal is pressed or released.**

- **When using a pedal, the bottom of your foot stays in contact with the pedal.** You should feel the pedal underneath your foot even when the pedal is released.

- **The damper pedal is used with the right foot while the soft and sostenuto pedals are used with the left foot.** If all three pedals are used simultaneously, the left foot presses the soft *and* sostenuto pedal with the front of the foot angled slightly toward the damper pedal while the right foot presses the damper pedal as usual.

Damper Pedal Depressed   **Damper Pedal Released**   Damper and Sostenuto Pedal Depressed

- **Do not suddenly release a pedal, causing mechanical noise or string vibration.** To demonstrate this, listen carefully to the difference between depressing the damper pedal quickly with a slow release and depressing that pedal slowly with a sudden release.

- **Do not lift the damper pedal all the way up when momentarily releasing or flipping that pedal.** Most pedals have some degree of play (see glossary) at the top of the pedal stroke. Your ear is the best judge of correct pedal movement.

Legato or "Syncopated" Pedaling: A commonly used damper pedal technique that allows a smooth, legato sound without blurring into the next notes. As your fingers press down the keys, your foot lifts up the damper pedal and immediately presses it back down.

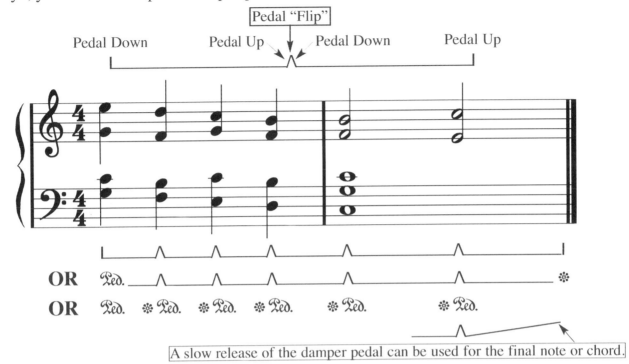

The following activity will help develop the coordination needed for legato pedaling.

1. **Play one key at a time from middle C up to G and back down to middle C, using fingers 1 through 5 in the right hand.** Do this very slowly.
2. **Begin flipping the damper pedal immediately after each new note.** Listen very carefully to see if any two notes are momentarily blurring. If they are, flip the pedal sooner and/or quicker. Be sure there are no gaps of silence between the notes. In your mind, think: "Note-flip, note-flip, note-flip, etc."
3. **Repeat these two steps with the left hand, moving from C down to F and back up.**
4. **As you become proficient, gradually raise the speed of your playing.**
   Use the metronome, if desired. Be sure no blurring occurs.

Additional Tips:
• Sometimes damper pedal markings are given for only a few measures and then cease to be indicated. In this case you are expected to continue pedaling in a similar manner (*Ped. simile*) or to pedal appropriately for that style of music.
• You can emphasize or stress notes by depressing the pedal at the same time as the notes rather than afterwards.
• Releasing the damper pedal slowly produces an interesting effect, especially in sections of music that gradually get softer or where one hand drops out.
• Different effects can be obtained by depressing the pedal to different levels.
For a thorough study of the pedals, read **The Pianist's Guide To Pedaling** by Joseph Banowetz (see bibliography).

Troubleshooting Rhythm

If you are having difficulty comprehending the duration of note values smaller than a quarter note (less than one beat), study the following topics as needed.

EIGHT NOTES AND RESTS

1. Write out the divisions of the beat above each note, as shown below.
- **+** is the word "and".
- The beats in the example below are counted "1 and 2 and 3 and 4 and".
- Since an eighth note is half of one beat, a single eighth note played *on* a beat number would be released on the "and" *of that beat*. An eighth note played on the "and" is released on the beat number that follows.

2. Count out loud until the duration of each note is correct and the beat is steady.
- Say the beat number when playing the note or rest that is *on* the beat.
- Say "and" when playing the note or rest *half way between* each beat, shown by the (+).

To check steadiness, use one or both of the following tips:
A. Use a metronome.
- The beat number is said *on* the tick.
- The "and" is said *half way between* each tick.

B. Tap your left foot.
- Touch the foot to the floor on the downbeat (the beat number or metronome tick).
- Pivot the foot up to the top of its stroke on the "and" or upbeat (precisely half way between each beat or tick).
- Move your foot at a steady pace.

If you are still having difficulty, do the following:
A. Set the metronome speed to double that of your current tempo. (If doubling the speed exceeds 208 b.p.m., just use 208.)
B. Play an eighth note on each consecutive metronome tick, saying "one" on the first tick, "and" on the second tick, "two" on the third tick, and so forth, until easy.
C. Divide the metronome speed in half (104 b.p.m., if 208 was the double).
D. Starting exactly on a tick, play eighth notes at the *same* pace you just played. Say the beat number on each tick and the "and" half way between each tick.
E. Count out loud until the duration of each note is correct and the beat is steady.

SIXTEENTH NOTES AND RESTS

1. Write out the divisions of the beat above each note, as shown below.
- **+** is the word "and".
- **e** is the long vowel "ee".
- **a** is the short vowel "uh".
- The example below is counted "1 ee and uh, 2 ee and uh, 3 ee and uh, 4 ee and uh".
- Since a sixteenth note is one-fourth of a beat, a single sixteenth note played *on a beat number* would be released on the "ee" *of that beat*, a sixteenth note played on the "ee" would be released on the "and" *of that beat*, and so on.

2. Count out loud until the duration of each note is correct and the beat is steady.
- Say the beat number when playing the note or rest that is *on* the beat.
- Say the words "ee and uh" when playing the note or rest on each respective point before the next beat.

To check steadiness, use one or both of the following tips:
A. Use a metronome.
- The beat number is said *on* the tick.
- The "and" is said *half way between* each tick.

B. Tap your left foot.
- Touch the foot to the floor on the downbeat (the beat number or metronome tick).
- Pivot the foot up to the top of its stroke on the "and" or upbeat (precisely half way between each beat or tick).
- Move your foot at a steady pace.

If you are still having difficulty, *yet understand eighth notes thoroughly,* do the following:
A. Set the metronome speed to double that of your current tempo. (If doubling the speed exceeds 208 b.p.m., just use 208.)
B. Consider each metronome tick as an eighth note. Play two sixteenth notes for each tick, as if playing two eighth notes for each quarter note beat. Say "one" on the first tick, "and" on the second tick with the "ee" and "uh" between every other tick, until easy.
C. Divide the metronome speed in half (104 b.p.m., if 208 was the double).
D. Starting exactly on a tick, play sixteenth notes at the *same* pace you just played. Say the beat number on each tick and the "ee and uh" on each respective point between the tick.
E. Count out loud until the duration of each note is correct and the beat is steady.

TRIPLETED EIGHTH NOTES AND RESTS

1. Write out the divisions of the beat above each note, as shown below.

- **e** is spoken as a long vowel "ee".
- **a** is spoken as the short vowel "uh".
- The example below is counted: "1 ee uh, 2 ee uh, 3 ee uh, 4 ee uh".
- Since a tripleted eighth note is one-third of a beat, a single tripleted eighth note played *on* a beat number would be released on the "ee" *of that beat*, a tripleted eighth note played on the "ee" would be released on the "uh" *of that beat* and so on.

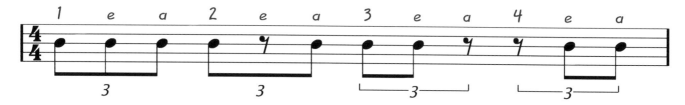

2. Count out loud until the duration of each note is correct and the beat is steady.

- Say the beat number when playing the note or rest that is *on* the beat.
- Say the words "ee uh" when playing the note or rest on each respective point before the next beat.

To check steadiness, use one or both of the following tips:

A. Use a metronome.

- The beat number is said *on* the tick.
- The "ee" is said *one-third* of the way through tick and the "uh" on the final third.

B. Tap your left foot.

- Touch the foot to the floor on the downbeat (the beat number or metronome tick).
- Raise the foot half-way up on the "ee".
- Continue raising the foot up until it reaches the top of its stroke on the "uh".

In other words, lift the foot in two even increments for the "ee uh" and then quickly drop the foot to the floor for the next beat number.

If you are still having difficulty, do the following:

A. Set the metronome speed to approximately triple that of your current tempo. (If tripling the speed exceeds 208 b.p.m., just use 208.)

B. Consider each metronome tick as a tripleted eighth note. Play tripleted eighth notes on each tick, saying "one" on the first tick, "ee" on the second tick, "uh" on the third tick, and so forth, until easy.

C. Divide the metronome speed by one-third (69 b.p.m., if 208 was the triple).

D. Starting exactly on a tick, play tripleted eighth notes at the *same* pace you just played. Say the beat number on each tick and the "ee uh" on each respective point between the tick.

E. Count out loud until the duration of each note is correct and the beat is steady.

Difficult Rhythm Changes

Below are various rhythms with the divisions of the beat printed above each note.

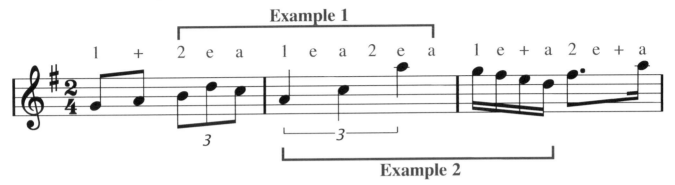

- In the second measure, each tripleted quarter note is divided into two syllables (1 e / a 2 / e a) for correct note placement.
- In the third measure, the dotted eighth note is counted as "2 e and", not "2 and" ensuring the following sixteenth note is struck at the correct time.

1. **Divide the beat by its smallest note.**
   If the smallest note in a beat is a sixteenth note, divide the beat by four.
   If the smallest note in a beat is an eighth note, divide the beat by two, and so on.
2. **Say or think all divisions of the given beat.** This helps keep the pace steady and prevents notes from being played prematurely.
3. **Practice transitioning between two difficult rhythms on a single key, gradually faster.**
   Example 1 can be reduced to the two rhythms below, for ease of practice. (This also provides the added benefit of practicing tripleted quarter notes into tripleted eighths.)

If the intended tempo is too fast for single-key strikes, use step-wise motion through the fingers, moving down toward the thumb. Example 2 could be practiced as shown below.

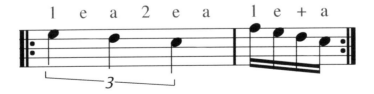

When the rhythm change becomes instinctual or a matter of feeling rather than thought, counting the divisions of the beat will no longer be required and the actual notes, fingering and expression can be used.

Polyrhythms - Method 1

Polyrhythms are different rhythms played at the same time, each rhythm having a different subdivision of the beats. Two common polyrhythms are shown below.

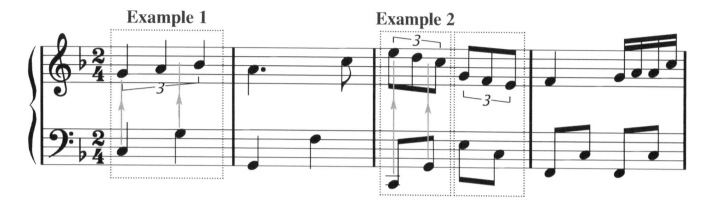

Tip:
Draw vertical lines from the longer note value to the shorter to show the sequence of keystrikes between the hands. Four such lines are shown above.

Example 1: Two beats are subdivided by three in the treble staff and by two in the bass staff. Three right hand notes are played evenly against two in the left.

Example 2: Each beat is subdivided by three in the treble staff and by two in the bass staff. Three right hand notes are again played evenly against two in the left.

The second example will be used to demonstrate Method 1.

1. **Apply Practice Routine, step 2.** The left hand starts with the easier eighth notes, then the right hand plays tripleted eighth notes. At the base tempo, continue playing each rhythm separately against quarter note ticks until you can play each rhythm with ease.

2. **Use a recording device to compare the rhythms against each other.**

    A. **At the base tempo, record yourself playing eighth notes for about one minute.**

    B. **Turn off the metronome and play *tripleted* eighth notes while listening to your recording.** Practice until your tripleted eighth notes are even against the recorded eighth notes.

    C. **At base tempo, record yourself playing tripleted eighth notes for about a minute.**

    D. **Turn off the metronome and play *eighth* notes while listening to your recording.** Practice until your eighth notes are even against the recorded tripleted eighth notes.

An alternative to step 2 is the following:

Use each metronome tick as one of the note values.

A. Double the base tempo and consider each tick to be the value of one eighth note (eighth note ticks). It is easier to start with the longer of the two note values in a polyrhythm. In this case it is the eighth note.

B. Play tripleted eighth notes against the eighth note ticks for about one minute. Although this alternative can produce fast results, it may be more difficult as you must *feel* the quarter note beats instinctively since they will not be indicated by the metronome. If needed, tap your foot on every quarter note (two ticks apart) to remind you where each group of three tripleted eighth notes begins.

Note:
If step 2 or its alternate are too difficult, repeat one or both steps clapping your hands and/or saying the subdivisions of the beat. When easy, return to the keyboard. When *either* step 2 or its alternate have been mastered on the keyboard, go on to step 3.

3. Play hands together slowly or at the base tempo, looping it over and over. Feel the smaller division of the beat. In this case, the tripleted eighth rhythm dominates over the eighth rhythm. Develop a feel for the sequence of the notes between the hands. Your goal is to be able to play both rhythms continuously without stopping. When ready, return to step 3 of the Practice Routine.

Polyrhythms - Method 2

The circled polyrhythm, below, will be used to demonstrate another approach to polyrhythms. Here, two beats are subdivided by four in the right hand and by three in the left hand (four right hand notes are played evenly against the three in the left).

1. **Find the lowest common denominator of both rhythms.** In this polyrhythm, there are 4 eighth notes against 3 tripleted quarter notes. The lowest common denominator of 4 and 3 is 12.

2. **Create a chart with the numbers 1 through 12 and place a line over each number where the right hand plays and a line underneath each number where the left hand plays.** This is shown below.

```
R.H. ―              ―              ―              ―
        1   2   3   4   5   6   7   8   9   10   11   12
L.H. ―                  ―                  ―
```

3. **Place your index fingers on two keys of the same name in the middle of the keyboard.**

4. **With your right hand, count from 1 to 12 repeatedly, striking the key on the correct number with a very steady beat.**

5. **Repeat step 4 with the left hand.**

6. **Play the keys, hands together, on the correct numbers.** Count slowly and carefully.

7. **Set the metronome to a comfortable speed and begin looping through the numbers while playing.** Each tick represents a number on the chart.

8. **Gradually raise the metronome speed to 200 beats per minute.** At *each* speed, loop the 12 numbers continually while counting with the metronome, until easy.

9. **At 200 b.p.m., loop the 12 numbers continually until the rhythm is instinctual, without the need to count.**

10. **Divide the speed in half (100 b.p.m.). Loop the 12 numbers until the rhythm is instinctual, without the need to count.** Each metronome tick represents an eighth note and occurs on every third number (1, 4, 7 and 10).

11. **Divide this speed in half (50 b.p.m.). Loop the 12 numbers until the rhythm is instinctual, without the need to count.** Each metronome tick represents a quarter note and occurs on every sixth number (1 and 7). This now coincides with the correct beat of the music which is the quarter note, since the time signature is $\frac{4}{4}$.

This method is suitable when the common denominator is 15 or less. Larger denominators are too laborious to count and the speeds necessary to give you a solid feel for the polyrhythm are too difficult to keep track of.

Sight-Reading

Sight-reading means to perform music at first sight, without practice on the instrument. Because the music is performed (not practiced), *all* aspects of the music are attempted such as rhythm, dynamics, pedaling, expression and so on. Sight-reading forces the eyes away from the keyboard which, over time, increases tactile awareness, improves distance judgement in the hands and speeds the learning of new music.

Sight-read for several minutes at a time, before or after each practice session. A variety of musical material should be sight-read as this opens the door to new discoveries and directions of interest and ultimately the selection of new and invigorating repertoire.

When sight-reading, keep the following points in mind.

- **Choose music below your current ability level.**

- **Note the key signature(s) and identify the correct scale(s) for the piece.**
  Knowledge of these scales instinctively provides immediate fingering solutions.

- **Identify the time signature to understand how the music is counted.**

- **Look over the music for other elements that might facilitate your performance such as intervals, chords and cadences (a series of chords bringing a section to an end).**

- **Consider your tempo carefully.** If necessary, play slower than the stated tempo so errors do not interrupt the flow of the music.

- **Play as many of the musical details as possible with hands together, keeping a steady beat.**

- **Concentrate on the melody and the bass line, capturing inner parts as much as possible.**

- **Keep your eyes on the music, ahead of where the hands are currently playing.**
  Your eyes lead your hands by no less than two beats.

- **Do not stop to correct mistakes.**

- **If necessary, omit notes in a rapid passage or large chord to maintain the flow.**

- **Do not play any one piece more than two times as you will defeat the purpose of sight-reading.**

Scale and Chord Drills

To master all scales and chord types wherein you can instantly recognize and play them in any key, use the following drill.

1. **Select the scale or chord type to be drilled.**

2. **Establish fingering for that scale or chord type.** Correct scale fingering can be found in **Essential Keyboard Technique**, available at www.wehrlipubs.com or selected retailers. Correct chord fingering is determined by hand size and is typically 1, 3, 5 or 1, 2, 4 for 3-note chords (triads) and 1, 2, 3, 5 for 4-note chords (tetrads).

3. **Practice the scale or chord type in all keys, hands separately, moving chromatically up and down one octave.** As you play each scale or individual chord, say its name out loud or silently. This connects a name to the physical action on the keyboard. See Chromatic Example, below.

4. **Practice the same scale or chord type in all keys, hands separately, moving through the Circle of 5ths.** Again, say the name of each scale or individual chord as you play. See Circle of 5ths Example, below.

5. **When steps 3 and 4 can be played without hesitation or error, practice these steps *slowly* with your eyes closed, thinking each name.** This strengthens your visualization of the keyboard.

6. **Play the scale or chord sequence hands together with your eyes open.**

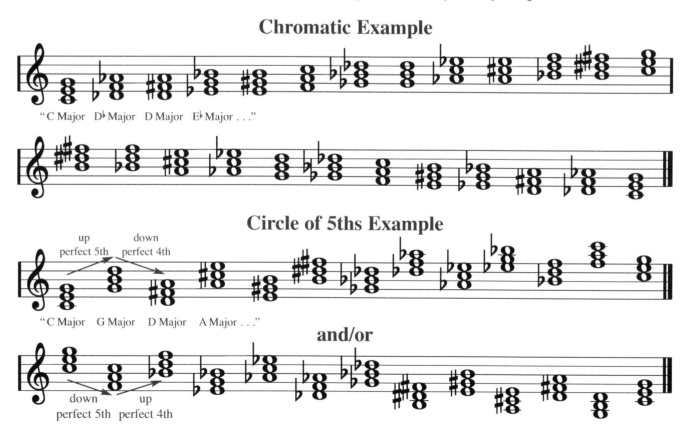

Piano Practice and Performance

Chapter 4

Memorization

Memorization has been known to increase intellect and mental acuity. The ancient Greek Academies required rhetorical and musical studies to be memorized for performance.

Memorization allows you to listen to what you are playing with minimal distraction. The visual and mental demands of reading music often overshadow the precise awareness of touch, movement and sound. When the eyes are no longer dependent on the score, the mind and ear can work together to direct physical movements toward the desired sound. With the piece in your mind, you can better focus on details such as voice balance, sound projection, body movement and tempo changes, refining them to your goals.

Memorization cannot be forced or rushed. It occurs naturally from repeating the same activity many times. The number of repetitions needed depends on the individual, the type of memorization (analytical, visual, aural or tactile) and the difficulty of the piece. Try not to be too hard on yourself if memorization does not come as quickly as you thought it might. You are developing both physical and mental perceptions; recognize and enjoy the achievements made along the way.

MEMORIZATION PREPARATIONS

1. **Use the 3X Rule and Practice Routine to learn your piece accurately.** This reduces the risk of accidentally memorizing mistakes. When you can play the piece easily and accurately, you are ready to memorize it as a whole.
2. **Divide the piece into sections.** A section is a phrase or quantity of a piece that gives a sense of momentary pause, like a sentence. It is easier to memorize a section at a time, connecting them as you go. If the piece is complicated, memorize one or two measures at a time, instead.

THE FOUR TYPES OF MEMORY

ANALYTICAL MEMORY

Analytical memory is using music theory (patterns, relationships and functions) to analyze and understand the music.

Recognize as many of the following elements as possible:
- **Form (binary is 2 sections, ternary is 3 sections, sonata movements and so on).**
- **Tonality (key) and subsequent modulations (key changes).**
- **Motives or "motifs" (short, recurring musical ideas) and how they vary.**
- **Melodic phrase structures (question and answer, imitation, repetition, sequence).**
- **Cadences (authentic or V-I, half or I-V, plagal or IV-I and so on).**
- **Chord progressions (series of chords, as related to the current key or scale).**
- **Chord structures and their inversions (positions or arrangement of notes).**
- **Intervals (the distances or relationships between notes).**

TACTILE MEMORY

Tactile memory is remembering the hand and finger movements on the keyboard.

1. A. Pick one hand and play the selected section two times, looking at the music.
   B. Play it a third time with your eyes closed. If you have difficulty, repeat step 1A until you can play it with your eyes closed. Do not simply look away from the music. Close your eyes so you can feel the distance between the keys being played, the amount of pressure the fingers are using to play the keys and the hand shapes used in that section. Start with a couple of measures at a time and build up to the full section.
2. Repeat step 1 with the other hand.
3. Repeat step 1 with both hands.
4. Continue steps 1-3 for each section. Although you do not need to be able to play the entire piece with your eyes closed, your tactile memory should be developed enough so that you feel you *could* do so.

AURAL MEMORY

Aural memory is hearing the music in your mind.

1. A. Pick one hand and play the chosen section of the score.
   B. Hear how that hand sounds in your mind, or hum it out loud. If you have difficulty, play the section again until you can hear it in your mind. Start with a few measures at a time and build up to the full section.
   C. Close your eyes and recall how that hand in the selected section sounds without looking at the music. If you have difficulty, play the music. If you still cannot hear it, play it until you remember how it sounds without the music.
2. Repeat step 1 with the other hand.
3. Repeat step 1 with both hands.
4. Continue steps 1-3 for each section.

VISUAL MEMORY

Visual memory is picturing the score in your mind.

1. A. Pick one hand and view the chosen section of the score.
   B. Close your eyes and picture what you just viewed. If you have difficulty, review the section and try again until you can see it in your mind. Start with a couple of measures at a time and build up to the full section.
2. Repeat step 1 with the other hand.
3. Repeat step 1 with both hands, without looking at the music.
4. Continue steps 1-3 for each section.

TIPS DURING MEMORIZATION

- **Keep fingering consistent.** Tactile memory is stored in the fingers. Changing fingering after memorizing a piece "erases" the tactile memory.

- **In areas with similar material, make note of the differences.** For example, recognizing that "the key is D Major the first time and A Major the second" or that "the melody is played an octave higher the second time", aids memorization.

- **At each practice session, begin memorizing a new section of the piece first, before reviewing previously-memorized sections.** This maintains forward progress and prevents procrastination.

- **As each new section is memorized, join it to the previous one.** Rehearse the measures connecting the two sections using any of the four types of memorization, if needed.

- **Alternating-hand patterns should be learned and memorized hands together.** Fit these patterns into the sections being memorized hands separately. For example, the right hand begins the given section, the left hand joins in for the pattern and then exits while the right hand continues.

- **During memorization, stop occassionally to *read* through the entire score.** This will refresh you on the overall intent and form of the piece and remind you of important details.

TIPS AFTER MEMORIZATION

- **If a memory lapse occurs, quickly review the area, starting from a point just before the memory lapse to just after. Once your review is complete, continue playing by memory from there on.** Do not start again from the beginning.

- **Start at various sections or phrases and play to the end, by memory.** Do this at the piano and if possible, in your mind. (See Strengthening Memorization for details.)

- **Occasionally read the music while playing.** This strengthens your visual memory and ensures that all markings in the music have been captured.

- **Try playing the entire piece hands separately, by memory.** Although this takes some effort, it further improves tactile memory and, during a memory slip, provides the security of having one hand able to continue on while the other catches up.

Strengthening Memorization

Once you have memorized the piece, that memory needs to be secured. The following two techniques (often neglected in musical training) strengthen memorization.

1. **Training away from the piano with the music.** Hear the performance in your mind, away from the piano, as you follow the score. This first technique severs the physical connection to and dependency on your instrument for memorization.

2. **Training away from the piano without the music.** In your mind, hear and see your performance at the keyboard with complete detail, expression and emotion. This second technique requires considerable concentration to be beneficial.

The above techniques provide:

- **Total comprehension and assimilation.** Playing the piece in your mind brings together all musical aspects as a flowing expression regardless of any difficulties that may remain in playing the piece; tempo limitations due to technical difficulties are abandoned, leaps across the keyboard occur without delay and melodies soar over the accompaniment regardless of their register.

- **Security in performance.** When you can accurately see and hear the keys being played in your mind, you *know* the piece. This awareness builds the ultimate in performance confidence.

Tip:
These two techniques can also be used after step 9 of the Practice Routine (page 17) to strengthen the learning process. Directly after a section has been learned accurately at the keyboard, sit down elsewhere and hear that section in your mind while reading the score or visualizing the keyboard. If you have difficulty, return to the piano and play the section again to "record" it, both visually and sonically; then try again. However, do not exhaust yourself with memorization after step 9; each section learned using the Practice Routine is subsequently played many times over as the piece is further practiced, allowing natural memorization to occur.

Performance Timeline

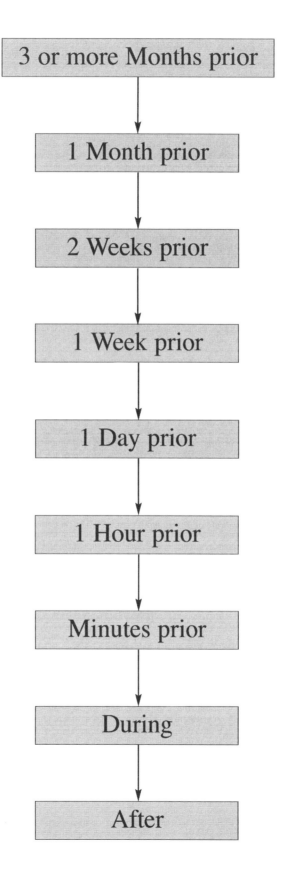

Performance Routine

Performance, whether in the concert hall or the living room, demands (1) mastery of the music, (2) good presence in front of the audience and (3) proper perspective. Follow the routine below to achieve these goals.

THREE OR MORE MONTHS PRIOR

1. Select music that is:
- **At or slightly below your ability level,** *not above*.
- **Not longer than your concentration or attention span.**
- **Of a comfortable length, allowing sufficient time to have properly learned the entire piece or program** *one month* **before the performance.**
- **Meaningful to you, encouraging expression and communication to an audience.**

2. Prepare steadily and thoroughly. Procrastination = lower confidence and higher anxiety.

ONE MONTH PRIOR

1. Play straight through the entire piece or program. Do not stop for any mistakes. This provides the benefits of:
- Training you to continue past any possible mistakes during the performance.
- Giving you a feel for how much energy and strength will be required to perform your piece or program.
- Indicating the areas that still need refinement.

2. Obtain a speed slightly higher than the actual performance tempo. Once this speed is mastered, return to the correct tempo. Play at the higher speed on occasion. This reduces the risk of performance problems should you accidentally play faster due to nerves. It also makes the performance tempo comparatively easier and helps avoid the anxiety of being pushed to your limits during performance.

3. For possible encores, select repertoire complimentary to your program. Refine these pieces through consistent, light practice.

4. Make all other performance arrangements. Projects may include speech preparation, travel plans, hiring a caterer, technician or assistant, printing programs, and so on.

TWO WEEKS PRIOR

1. Get an objective view of your progress by doing both of the following:
   A. Recording a couple of rehearsals and listening directly afterwards.
   B. Playing your piece or program for several objective listeners.
   Take notes while listening to your recording or selected audience commentary. Make necessary changes to your performance and repeat A and B until you are satisfied.

2. **Become accustomed to the clothing in which you will be performing.** If the performance requires formal attire, rehearse the entire program in that attire. Clothing of this type might be warmer or more restrictive than casual clothing. Any part of your attire that binds or constricts should be altered or replaced immediately. Do not wait until the performance to try on that tuxedo, suit or evening gown.

ONE WEEK PRIOR

1. **Rehearse your program from start to finish, recording yourself to catch if you are rushing due to nervousness.**

2. **Eat and sleep well the week (or at least two days) prior to the performance.** Avoid eating refined sugar which causes a sudden rise and fall in blood-sugar level, creating fatigue, muscle cramps and other related symptoms. Low blood-sugar levels can increase nervousness and anxiety. Eat healthy, natural carbohydrates or proteins that when metabolized, increase your endurance.

3. **If available, rehearse on the performance instrument.** This will give you a chance to adjust your keyboard and pedaling technique to that instrument. Playing this instrument onstage will benefit you even more; an attentive ear in this environment will govern precise adjustments in technique according to room acoustics (the way sound reflects off or is absorbed by its interior surfaces). If the instrument or venue is not available, rehearse on as many different pianos as possible to prepare for the eventuality of an unknown instrument; a piano store or music school might accommodate this request.

Important Note:
At this point no further changes should be made to the music, particularly fingering. Changes made this close to the performance will only weaken your "automatic pilot" and compromise your sense of security. Whatever slight imperfections remain, accept them fully.

4. **Confirm all arrangements and make final preparations.** These might include your transportation, the arrival times of various personnel, packing your programs and backstage items, and so forth.

ONE DAY PRIOR

1. **Sit in the house (where the audience sits) and visualize your performance on stage.** Experience the performance in your mind as the audience would if you were on stage at that moment. Use your Memorization Strengthening techniques to view both sides of a musical performance: that of the performer *and* of the audience.

2. **Rehearse the entire performance only once or twice.** Do not rehearse excessively, as this can produce fatigue lasting into tomorrow's performance and will only enlarge the significance of any remaining imperfections.

ONE HOUR PRIOR
Mental Preparation

1. **Accept nervousness and channel it to your advantage.** Performance and nervousness go hand-in-hand. Virtually every performer experiences it. Although the feeling is unpleasant, the tension of an approaching performance is energy that can be used to prevent failures and make a performance successful. Channel nervous energy towards your best interests. Take deep, refreshing breaths to keep muscles relaxed.

2. **Do not take yourself or a performance too seriously.** Think of the performance as "going to work", where you have the wonderful opportunity to converse with and teach the audience about the music you have prepared. You are not "on trial", even if you *are* performing in a competition.

3. **Do not seek perfection.** Some pianists carry the weight of the world on their shoulders because to them, their performances must be perfect. Remember, the more you perform, the better you will become *at* performing. The audience will remember how your performance made them *feel*, not how many mistakes you made.

MINUTES PRIOR

1. **Adjust any loose or tight clothing.**

2. **Be sure the fingers are warm and limber.** Any of the following can be done:
   • Use the Stretches and Warm-Ups on pages 10-12.
   • Immerse cold hands in warm water for about one minute.
   • Rub cold hands in front of an area heater.

3. **Be sure your hands are clean and oil-free.**

4. **Dry sweaty palms continually with a towel.** In extreme cases, apply a *light* coating of corn starch or antiperspirant to the palms *only*, making sure none comes in contact with the fingers.

5. **Determine if you should use the restroom.**

6. **Drink small quantities of water frequently to keep the body and mouth hydrated.** Nervousness can cause unpleasant dry-mouth.

7. **Just before you perform, breathe normally and steadily.** When feeling nervous, the tendency for shallow breathing reduces the amount of oxygen in the blood, making the muscles unsteady and more difficult to use.

DURING

1. **Smile when entering and leaving the stage.** Facial expression can convey nervousness, a condition the audience should not perceive.

2. **When you arrive in front of the piano (typically a position between the piano bench and the audience), acknowledge the audience applause with a full bow, not just a nod.** Deliver the prepared speech for that point on the program, if any.

3. **Sit on the piano bench and make any final adjustments to the bench height and location as well as your body and foot placement.**

4. **Before beginning, take a few deep, slow breaths and in your mind, do the following:**
   - **Hear the first few measures at the correct tempo and *not any faster*.**
   - **Establish the meaning and emotion of the music's entrance.**

5. **While performing, do not stop for any mistakes.** Continue playing and the audience may not notice. Make the ending a big success.

6. **Focus on the music so as not to be distracted by sounds or reactions in the audience.** Most people will sit quietly and be interested and appreciative during your performance. However, some might be tired, restless or squirm in their seat. Others might be ill and their coughing or sneezing could be distracting. Stay focused on the music to keep distractions from throwing you off.

7. **At the end of the piece or movement, do not lift your hands right away.** Lift the keys with only your fingertips, keeping your hands on the keyboard. Then lift your hands off the keyboard. If using the pedal, first lift the keys with your fingertips, then slowly lift the pedal, keeping your hands on the keyboard. When the pedal has silenced all sound, then lift your hands off the keyboard.

8. **No acknowledgement is necessary between movements.** Customarily, there is no applause between movements of a work so audience acknowledgement is not necessary. Should there be any applause between movements, you may nod *once* to the audience if you wish, but do not stand up. Wait for applause to cease, then begin the next movement.

9. **When you finish each *complete* work, stand up, face the audience and take a bow.** The audience should applaud only at the end of each *complete* work, at which point you stand and bow to the center or to each section of the audience (house-left, house-center, house-right). Look at and listen to the audience; as long as they steadily clap, continue to take slow bows. When the applause begins to die down, deliver the next speech, if any. Then prepare for the next piece on your program per steps 3-9.

10. **At the end of your final piece, stand, take slow bows and then begin to walk off the stage (do not rush) while the applause is still strong.**

11. Once backstage, one of two situations will occur:

- **The applause will die out.** If so, remain backstage and prepare to meet guests.
- **The applause will continue, possibly growing louder with interjections by the audience. If so, show your appreciation.** Performers should have additional repertoire ready for possible encores. If you have no other repertoire to offer, choose a piece from your program that you think the audience might like to hear again. Perform your encore piece per steps 1-9 on the previous page.

  The following sequence of actions is *suggested*:

  A. **Return to the stage to perform an encore.**

  B. **After you finish your encore, stand, take slow bows, and again walk off the stage while the applause is still strong.**

  C. **If the applause continues or grows louder while backstage, decide if you should perform another encore. If so, repeat A-C.**

  D. **If the applause persists and you are exhausted of (from) encores, return to the stage one last time for a curtain call.** In this case, calm the audience by speaking your words of appreciation to bring the performance to a close.

AFTER

- **Backstage or at a reception, greet your guests with a smile and good cheer.** The quality of your performance has no bearing on how you treat those that took the time to see you perform. Be gracious and appreciative.

- **Be prepared to handle all post-performance responsibilities.** Such tasks might include paying your assistants, packing your belongings, removing signage, and so forth.

- **Do not over-analyze immediately after your performance.** Consider it in greater detail the next day.

- **If possible, rest the next day.** Performing can be mentally and physically taxing. The following day, regain your strength by sleeping in and avoiding strenuous activities.

- **Assess your performance with constructive criticism.** Instead of fixating on weaknesses, flaws or mistakes, recognize what needs improvement and what does not. Each performance is an opportunity to learn and grow; take what you have learned from the experience and use it to improve future performances. (See below.)

- **Complete a Performance Assessment Sheet for each work performed.** Reflecting on the piece performed and writing your evaluation on paper provides both an objective review and ideas for possible improvements. Keep Performance Assessment sheets on file as a record of improvement over time. Keep blank copies on hand for future use.

- **Maintain this repertoire.** One or more works may be used for future programs or encores.

- **As stated before, the more you perform, the better you will become *at* performing.**

Piano Practice and Performance
··
Performance Assessment Sheet

Work or Movement Title:_____

Composer:_____   Edition or Arranger:_____

Performance Date:_____   Performance Venue:_____

Piano Make:_____   Model:_____   Size:_____

Keyboard Action (even, uneven, heavy, light, etc.):_____

Pedal Action (loose, sticky, shallow, etc.):_____

Venue Acoustics (bright, dull, reverberant, etc.):_____

Answer the following question for each point below. Note their location in the score.

Were there inaccuracies in:

Notes Played ❑NO ❑YES - location(s)_____

_____

Rhythm ❑NO ❑YES - location(s)_____

_____

Tempi ❑NO ❑YES - location(s)_____

_____

Dynamics ❑NO ❑YES - location(s)_____

_____

Voice Balance ❑NO ❑YES - location(s)_____

_____

Articulation ❑NO ❑YES - location(s)_____

_____

Pedaling ☐NO ☐YES - location(s)_____

_____

Interpretation ☐NO ☐YES - location(s)_____

_____

Other _____ ☐NO ☐YES - location(s)_____

_____

_____

Answer the following question for each point below. Circle the number that applies.

On a scale of 1 to 5 (five being best), how well did you:

Prepare this work:	1	2	3	4	5
Present your speech (if applicable):	1	2	3	4	5
Continue past mistakes without interruption:	1	2	3	4	5
Focus on the music:	1	2	3	4	5
Handle any nervousness:	1	2	3	4	5
Express your interpretation:	1	2	3	4	5
Adjust your playing to venue acoustics:	1	2	3	4	5
Acknowledge audience applause:	1	2	3	4	5

What was your single weakest point in performing this work?_____

_____

What was your single strongest point?_____

_____

Do you wish to keep this piece in your repertoire? ☐NO ☐YES
If so, what will you do to improve or maintain it? If not, why?_____

_____

Piano Practice and Performance

Glossary

Accent - Playing a note or chord louder than its surroundings.

Arrangement - An adaptation of a musical work to instruments for which it was not originally designed, or for some other use for which it was not at first written.

Articulation - The manner in which keys are played and then released; markings that show how to perform a musical note. Staccato and legato are examples.

Bagatelle - A French word used by Beethoven to describe a short piece, often for piano.

Base Tempo - The speed at which you can play with no errors on the *first* try.

Chord - A combination of three or more notes played at the same time.

Chromatically; Chromatic - A series of notes that are a half step apart.

Circle of 5ths - A circular arrangement of the twelve key or scale names in the order of ascending or descending perfect 5ths. After moving through these 12 keys, the initial key is reached again.

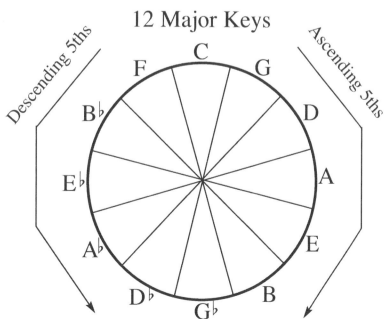

12 Major Keys

Crescendo - An indication in music that tells the performer to gradually play louder.

Curtain Call - An appearance by the performer in response to continued applause.

Damper - A small felt block which stops the vibrations of the piano strings for a particular key. When you press and release a key, the damper for that key stops the vibrations of its strings.

Dynamics - That aspect of music relating to volume; loudness or softness.

Encore - An additional, unscheduled piece played in response to enthusiastic applause.

Expression - The qualities in music which produce emotion and feeling such as degrees of loudness, changes in speed, touch of the keys, use of the pedals, and so on.

Fingering - The determination of which fingers are to be used in playing the keys. This is indicated by numbers written closely to the designated notes. For each hand, finger 1 is the thumb with fingers 2 through 5 spreading out to the pinky finger respectively.

Flat - A symbol (♭) that lowers the pitch of a note by a half step. See pages 22, 26 and 37 for examples of how flats appear in music.

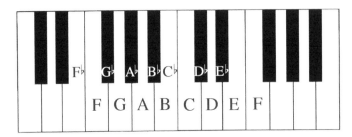

Flipping - From a depressed state, letting up the pedal and then instantly pressing it back down again. This is done quickly with minimal foot motion.

Form - The organization and structure of the sections in a work or movement.

Half step - A movement (up or down) to the nearest black or white key.

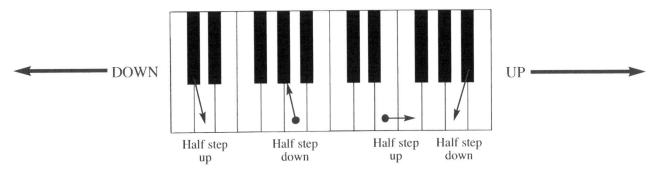

Improvisation - The art of creating music spontaneously during performance, without rehearsal or preparation. It is often based on some subject, theme, or idea.

Key - The center or main note in a musical composition that reflects which scale is used. The tonic (first) note of a scale is called the "key note". Keys can change within a work.

Key Signature - Sharp or flat symbols placed in front of the time signature that show which notes in the music are sharp or flat. It identifies the scale of the piece.

Legato - Played smoothly without gaps or interruptions between the notes.

Looping - Repeating again and again until a certain condition or state is achieved.

Metronome - A device that makes a steady ticking sound, like a clock. It assists in keeping track of the beats in music. The speed of the ticks is adjustable by a numeric scale based on the number of beats per minute.

Movement - Any of the complete and relatively independent sections within certain musical compositions. Usually there is a short pause between them. Each movement tends to feel like a separate musical statement, although a common idea or convention may be used throughout.

Octave - The distance of 12 half steps between a given note to the next note of the same name. The keyboard shown in the Flats definition illustrates an octave from the first F to the next consecutive F with 12 half steps between them.

Perfect 4th - The distance of 5 half steps between two notes.

Perfect 5th - The distance of 7 half steps between two notes.

Phrasing - The use of various expressions to produce a musical thought. A phrase ends at a point of stability and gives the listener a feeling that a "statement" has been made.

Piano - An Italian word that means "soft"; quietly. Its dynamic mark is *p*.

Piano Desk - The area of the piano where music is placed for reading during performance.

Pitch - How high or low a sound is. The pitch goes up or gets higher as you move to the right on the keyboard. The pitch goes down or gets lower as you move to the left on the keyboard. Pitch has nothing to do with loudness or softness.

Play - The amount of free movement in a mechanism before its functions are engaged.

Posture - Position or way of placing the body.

Program - Collectively, the compositions and other activities scheduled for performance; a printed listing of such, made available to the public.

Repertoire - Compositions previously learned and currently maintained for performance; pieces needing minimal preparation to be performance-ready.

Rhythm - Any sound characterized by regularly recurring strong and weak beats; the regular pulsation of music.

Roll - Playing the notes of a chord one after the other instead of simultaneously. Rolls move in one direction through the chord notes. They can start at the bottom and move up or start at the top and move down. Also called Arpeggio.

Scale - Whole steps and/or half steps arranged in a certain order within an octave. A scale is named by the note on which it starts. The C Major scale starts on C and has the following pattern of whole steps and half steps: whole–whole–half–whole–whole–whole–half. The scale used in a musical composition determines its "key".

Score - The printed notation of a musical composition.

Sharp - A symbol (♯) that raises the pitch of a note by a half step. See pages 22, 24 and 37 for examples of how sharps appear in music.

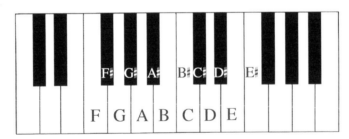

Sight read - To perform music at first sight, without practice on the instrument.

Slur - A curved line placed above or below a group of notes indicating they are to be played smoothly with no gaps or breaks between them.

Staccato - Short, detached, separated; a dot placed above or below a note indicating the key should be held for about one-half of its full value, depending on the music and taste.

Staff - A set of five equally spaced horizontal lines. Notes are written on the lines or in the surrounding spaces. The word *staff* can mean something that gives support. In music, a staff supports the notes. (See illustration on next page.)

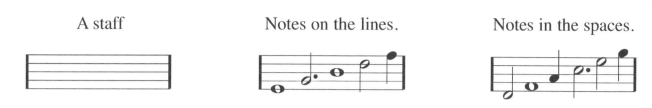

A staff   Notes on the lines.   Notes in the spaces.

Technique - Exercises, drills, or patterns designed to improve dexterity, strength, and independence in the fingers or other parts of the body; technical skills (in contrast to interpretational or expressive skills).

Tempo - The speed of a musical piece or passage; the speed of musical beats. The plural is either "tempi" or "tempos".

Tempo Mark - The musical term used to show the range of speed or pace of the music. It is written at the beginning of and possibly later in the work.

Time Signature - A sign that measures or counts beats in music. It is written as one number on top of another. The time signature indicates how many beats fit in one measure and what type of note gets one beat.

3 - There are 3 beats in each measure.
4 - The quarter note gets *one* beat.
   The "4" stands for the quarter note.

In other words, 3 quarter notes can fit in each measure.

Urtext - Music printed in its presumed original state, without additions or changes made by an editor.

Virtuoso - A performer who excels in technical ability and musicianship.

Voice Balance - The relative loudness or presence of each part (voice) in the music; typically, the emphasis of dominant melodic material over supporting accompaniment.

Whole step - A movement (up or down) of 2 half steps. 1 whole step = 2 half steps.

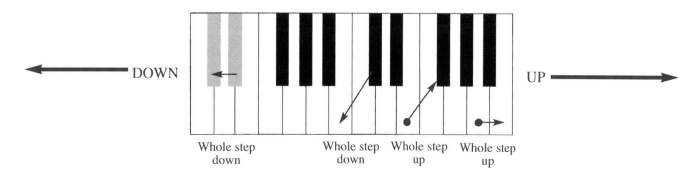

DOWN   UP

Whole step   Whole step   Whole step   Whole step
down   down   up   up

Piano Practice and Performance

Bibliography

Banowetz, Joseph. <u>The Pianist's Guide To Pedaling</u>. Bloomington: Indiana University Press, 1985.

Bastien, James W. <u>How To Teach Piano Successfully</u>. San Diego: Neil A. Kjos Music Company, 1988.

Berenson, Gail, et al. <u>A Symposium for Pianists and Teachers: Strategies to Develop the Mind and Body for Optimal Performance</u>. Ohio: Heritage Music Press, 2002.

Berman, Boris. <u>Notes From The Pianist's Bench</u>. New Haven: Yale University Press, 2000.

Bernstein, Seymour. <u>With Your Own Two Hands</u>. New York: Macmillan Publishing Company, Inc., 1981.

Chase, Mildred Portney. <u>Just Being At The Piano</u>. Culver City: Peace Press, Inc., 1981.

Harder, Paul O. <u>Harmonic Materials in Tonal Music, Part 1</u>. 5th ed. Newton: Allyn and Bacon, Inc., 1985.

Hofmann, Josef. <u>Piano Playing: With Piano Questions Answered</u>. New York: Dover Publications, Inc., 1976.

Neuhaus, Heinrich. <u>The Art of Playing The Piano</u>. New York: Praeger Publishers, Inc., 1973.

Newman, William S. <u>The Pianist's Problems</u>. New York: Harper & Bros. Publishers, 1956.

Novello, John. <u>The Contemporary Keyboardist</u>. Miami: CPP Belwin, 1987.

Randel, Don Michael. The <u>Harvard Concise Dictionary of Music and Musicians</u>. Cambridge: Harvard University Press, Belknap Press, 1999.

Schaum, Wesley. <u>Schaum Dictionary of Musical Terms</u>. Milwaukee: Schaum Publications, Inc., 1980.

Slenczynska, Ruth. <u>Music at Your Fingertips</u>. New York: Doubleday and Company, Inc., 1961.

Stretches and Warm-ups Consultation

Dr. Ric Alexander, D.C. California.

Dr. Jerry Brady, D.C. Washington.

Piano Practice and Performance
Instructor's Suggestions

More Cutting-Edge Books and Products
for the Music Teacher and Retailer

Essential Piano and Keyboard Technique

- Takes early-intermediate students well into advanced levels.
- Four sections present technical exercises by type or category for easy reference.
- Contains a variety of important technical exercises in addition to the traditional scales, chords, arpeggios and cadences.
- Numerous tips on using dynamics and articulation in technical exercises.
- Exceeds the technical requirements of many state and national programs.
- 8.125 x 10.5 perfect bound, 156 pages.

"If you want a comprehensive compendium of exercises that help build almost every aspect of technique, Essential Piano and Keyboard Technique is it. This book is a treasure trove. . . logically arranged into 4 broad sections for ease of locating specific exercises. Great resource!"
Patsy Rabinowitz - NCTM; Owner, West Chester Academy of Music.

Classic Series: Volume 1 Beginning Basics for the Piano

- A holistic approach for the beginning piano student, ages seven and up.
- Five workshops guide the student from learning the names of the white keys on the keyboard through playing beginner-level arrangements of famous works by Bach, Beethoven, Mozart as well as American classics.
- Posture, ear training and sight-reading projects develop skills needed to play easily and beautifully.
- 8.5 x 11 spiral bound, 204 pages including 12 flashcard pages.

". . . you have done an excellent job of presenting your ideas. Teachers could use your materials to enhance their teaching. It is clear that you have thought out things carefully and presented them in a systematic way that is helpful to both teachers and students."
Dr. Jeanine Jacobson - clinician and author of *Professional Piano Teaching*.

Classic Series: Volume 2 Intermediate Basics for the Piano

- A holistic approach that follows *Volume 1*, for the early-intermediate student.
- Five workshops introduce the student to subjects such as key signatures and accidentals, pedaling, ledger line notation, more complex rhythms and harmony.
- Music by classical and modern composers is arranged to demonstrate each subject, increasing in texture and complexity as the student progresses.
- Technical workouts develop strength and coordination.
- 8.5 x 11 spiral bound, 224 pages including 22 flashcard pages.

". . . Volume 2's five workshops cover more complicated musical concepts [than Volume 1] in a comprehensive way that will help students' positive progress. I would strongly recommend this Series to young teachers and self-study adults."
Dr. Anna Krendel - piano instructor, CAPMT District IX Coordinator.

(over)

Mastering Intervals

- For intermediate to advanced keyboardists.
- Three workshops systematically develop mastery in reading, writing and hearing any interval, enhancing composition and improvisation skills.
- 15 analyzed musical excerpts provide additional music theory insight.
- Answer Manual now included.
- 8.125 x 10.5 perfect bound, 158 pages.

"Mastering Intervals. . . [provides] a solid foundation of interval knowledge and a leg up for all musical endeavors. This in-depth workbook will be a welcome addition to any musician's library. Congratulations on a well thought out book!"
Andy LaVerne - Professor of Jazz Piano at The University of Hartford, recording artist and author of *Chord Substitutions* and *Countdown To Giant Steps.*

Music Instruction Forms: 1-Year Journal

- For all instrumentalists at any level of instruction.
- A Weekly Practice Calendar establishes the student's practice days and times and the total hours to practice within the week.
- 52 Weekly Lesson Plans carry the student through a full year's study. These easy to use plans organize assignments by category and provide spaces for the sequence, duration and grading of each assignment.
- Four Quarterly Student Progress Reports assess the student's strengths and weaknesses, quarterly. Divided into eight study categories and a general comments section, these reports keep the student on track through the year.
- Completed Journals provide a running record of the student's progress.
- 8.5 x 11 spiral bound, 68 pages.

Ear Training: Middle C to C

- A companion compact disc (CD) to *The Classic Series Volumes 1 and 2* or for any musician looking to improve pitch recognition.
- Develops instant pitch recognition from piano middle C to the next C above.
- Each of the 14 ear training sessions adds one new pitch at a time, providing an easy learning curve.
- A pitch is given with ample time to guess the correct key name and the answer announced afterward.
- Listen in your car, at work or at home. No teacher or assistance needed.
- Over an hour of training time on one CD.

Visit us at www.wehrlipubs.com.

Wehrli Publications

Cutting-Edge Books and Products
for the Music Teacher and Retailer

12830 Burbank Boulevard, Box 204 Valley Village, CA 91607-1402

5223823R0

Made in the USA
Charleston, SC
16 May 2010